Kids of Character

I Am a Good

By Maria Nelson

Gareth Stevens
Publishing

Please visit our website, www.garethstevens.com. For a free color catalog of all our high-quality books, call toll free 1-800-542-2595 or fax 1-877-542-2596.

Nelson, Maria.
I am a good friend / by Maria Nelson.
   p. cm. — (Kids of character)
Includes index.
ISBN 978-1-4339-9018-2 (pbk.)
ISBN 978-1-4339-9019-9 (6-pack)
ISBN 978-1-4339-9017-5 (library binding)
1. Friendship—Juvenile literature. 2. Friendship in children—Juvenile literature. I. Nelson, Maria. II. Title.
BF723.F68 N45 2014
177.62—dc23

First Edition

Published in 2014 by
Gareth Stevens Publishing
111 East 14th Street, Suite 349
New York, NY 10003

Copyright © 2014 Gareth Stevens Publishing

Designer: Nicholas Domiano
Editor: Kristen Rajczak

Photo credits: Cover, p. 1 © iStockphoto.com/kali9; p. 5 Digital Vision/Thinkstock.com; p. 7 Sam Edwards/ OJO Images/Getty Images; p. 9 Ron Chapple Studios/Thinkstock.com; p. 11 Jupiterimages/StockImage/ Getty Images; p. 13 Lisa F. Young/Shutterstock.com; p. 15 Philip J Brittan/Photographer's Choice/Getty Images; p. 17 Karen Struthers/Shutterstock.com; p. 19 Nancy R. Choen/Digital Vision/Getty Images; p. 21 Fuse/Thinkstock.com.

Printed in the United States of America

CPSIA compliance information: Batch #CS13GS: For further information contact Gareth Stevens, New York, New York at 1-800-542-2595.

Contents

Boldface words appear in the glossary.

What's a Friend?

Friends are the special people we like to be around most. It's important to be a good friend to them. Someone who is a good friend is kind. They treat their friends as they would want to be treated.

A Listening Ear

Nick was unhappy because his family was moving. He told Ryan he didn't want to live in a different neighborhood. Nick said he was worried about starting at a new school. Ryan listened. He was being a good friend.

Gloria didn't understand her math worksheet. She told Padma how hard it was! Padma was good at math. She offered to help Gloria with the worksheet. Good friends help each other. Padma was being a good friend.

Always Sharing

When the lunch bell rang, Rashida realized she had forgotten her lunch. Danielle offered to split her lunch with Rashida. Danielle was a good friend because she shared with Rashida.

Peter got a new video game for his birthday. When Jack came over to his house, Peter let Jack play. They each tried to win. Because they took turns at the game, Peter and Jack were good friends to each other.

Ah-Choo!

Marti called Trish to ask how she was feeling. Trish had the flu! Marti told her she had extra copies of their homework to bring to Trish when she was better. Marti showed **concern** for Trish. She was a good friend.

Playtime

Patty's dad taught her to play chess. Doug wanted to learn. Patty brought out her **chess** set to show him how to use the board and pieces. Good friends teach each other new things. Patty was a good friend to Doug.

Katy and Lucy went to the park after school. They saw Roberto standing alone on the playground. They asked him to play with them. Katy and Lucy showed how to be good friends. Good friends are happy to **include** others.

Tyler and Amelia are on the same soccer team. They have fun running together and **passing** the ball. One of the most important parts of being a friend is having a good time together. Tyler and Amelia are good friends!

Glossary

chess: a game for two players in which 16 pieces are moved around a checkered board

concern: a caring interest

include: to take in as part of a group

passing: kicking a ball to another person

For More Information

Books

Greve, Meg. *Friends*. Vero Beach, FL: Rourke Publishing, 2013.

Simon, Norma. *All Kinds of Friends*. Chicago, IL: Albert Whitman, 2012.

Websites

It's My Life: Friends

pbskids.org/itsmylife/friends/index.html
Learn about dealing with many situations between friends and others.

Kids Health: Friendship

www.cyh.com/HealthTopics/HealthTopicDetailsKids.aspx?p=335&np=286&id=1636
Read more about friendship on this kids-only website.

Index